THREE SHEETS IN THE WIND

THREE SHEETS IN THE WIND

thelwell's

MANUAL OF SAILING

EYRE METHUEN LTD

First published in 1973
by Eyre Methuen Ltd
11 New Fetter Lane, London EC4P 4EE
Copyright © 1973 by Norman Thelwell
Reprinted 1973

SBN 413 30610 0

Printed in Great Britain
by Fletcher & Son Ltd, Norwich

CONTENTS

GUY ROPE (CAPTAIN)

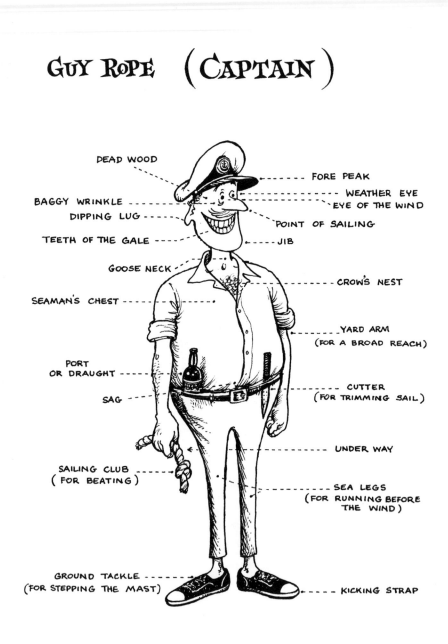

DEAD WOOD

FORE PEAK

WEATHER EYE

EYE OF THE WIND

BAGGY WRINKLE

DIPPING LUG

POINT OF SAILING

TEETH OF THE GALE

JIB

GOOSE NECK

CROW'S NEST

SEAMAN'S CHEST

YARD ARM
(FOR A BROAD REACH)

PORT
OR DRAUGHT

SAG

CUTTER
(FOR TRIMMING SAIL)

UNDER WAY

SAILING CLUB
(FOR BEATING)

SEA LEGS
(FOR RUNNING BEFORE
THE WIND)

GROUND TACKLE
(FOR STEPPING THE MAST)

KICKING STRAP

MAY DAY (FIRST MATE)

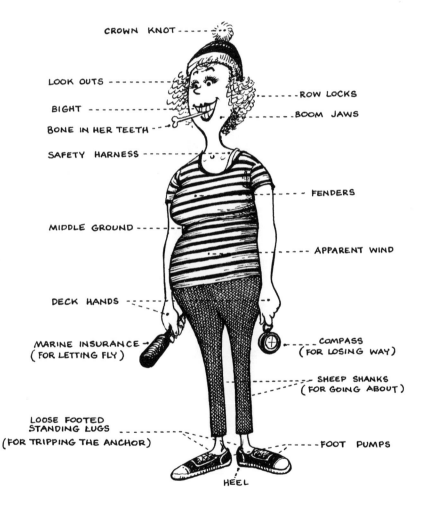

CROWN KNOT

LOOK OUTS

BIGHT

BONE IN HER TEETH

SAFETY HARNESS

MIDDLE GROUND

DECK HANDS

MARINE INSURANCE
(FOR LETTING FLY)

LOOSE FOOTED
STANDING LUGS
(FOR TRIPPING THE ANCHOR)

ROW LOCKS

BOOM JAWS

FENDERS

APPARENT WIND

COMPASS
(FOR LOSING WAY)

SHEEP SHANKS
(FOR GOING ABOUT)

FOOT PUMPS

HEEL

TECHNICAL TERMS

ENTERING UP THE LOG

A SAILOR'S BUNK

A SEA SHANTY

FREE BOARD

CAPSIZE

PERSONAL BUOYANCY

REEF POINTS

FLINDER'S BAR

LASHING DOWN

LOSING WAY

BOOM

A WINDLASS

DRESSED OVERALL

MAKING SAIL

A SAILING HORSE

TIDE RACE

NAVIGATION MARKS

BY AND LARGE

LYING IN THE ROADS

THE PLIMSOLL MARK

*　　*　　*

" WHERE'S THIS PLACE, MATE ? "

THE CALL OF THE SEA

SAILING IS THE FASTEST GROWING PARTICIPATION SPORT OF MODERN TIMES

IT IS NO LONGER THE EXCLUSIVE PRESERVE OF THE VERY RICH

NOR DOES ONE HAVE TO BE WEALTHY TO OWN ONE'S OWN CRAFT

SAILING IS A FAMILY SPORT

THERE IS NO ROOM FOR THE GENERATION GAP IN A BOAT

WHETHER YOUR PREFERENCE IS FOR THE FEEL OF A CAPRICIOUS BREEZE IN YOUR CANVAS —

OR FOR THE HEADY EXCITEMENT OF A SURGING POWER BOAT —

WHETHER YOU FIND YOURSELF DRAWN IRRESISTIBLY TO THE OPEN SEA —

OR TAKE YOUR PLEASURE IN INLAND WATERS , . . .

THERE IS NOTHING QUITE LIKE THE THRILL . . .

OF BEING IN SOLE COMMAND OF YOUR OWN BOAT.

* * *

" I'M **NOT** GOING TO BE RESCUED BY BOB AND VERA HARRINGTON."

SAFETY FIRST

MAKE SURE THAT YOUR VESSEL IS SEAWORTHY BEFORE SETTING SAIL

MAKE SURE THAT EACH MEMBER OF YOUR CREW IS WEARING A LIFE JACKET

AVOID WEIRS

DO NOTHING THAT MAY ALARM OR ANNOY BATHERS

ALWAYS STEP RIGHT INTO THE CENTRE OF A SMALL BOAT

ALWAYS CARRY ENOUGH FUEL — IT IS DIFFICULT TO OBTAIN AT SEA

AND NEVER MAKE ANY SIGNALS THAT MAY BE MISTAKEN FOR A DISTRESS CALL

LISTEN CAREFULLY TO WEATHER FORECASTS
AND ABOVE ALL....

GIVE YOUR FRIENDS ON SHORE PRECISE DETAILS OF WHERE
YOU INTEND TO SAIL

*   *   *

"I DON'T KNOW WHAT IT MEANS BUT IT'S A FOUR-LETTER WORD."

THE INTERNATIONAL CODE OF SIGNALS

I AM UNDERGOING A SPEED TRIAL

MAN OVERBOARD

I REQUIRE A TUG

STOP YOUR VESSEL
I HAVE SOMETHING IMPORTANT TO COMMUNICATE

I AM MANOEUVRING WITH DIFFICULTY

I AM IN NEED OF A PILOT

THIS VESSEL IS ABOUT TO DEPART

COMMUNICATE WITH ME

STOP CARRYING OUT YOUR INTENTIONS

I HAVE LOST MY BATHING COSTUME

✳   ✳   ✳

" A CURSE ON THAT SELF-STEERING GEAR."

Rules of the Road for Sailors

CLEAN OFF ALL BARNACLES – THEY WILL SLOW DOWN YOUR PROGRESS

KEEP WELL CLEAR OF ROCKS WHEN LEAVING HARBOUR

ORGANISE THE DOG WATCH

CHECK YOUR CRAFT FOR STOWAWAYS

BEWARE OF UNDERTOW

BE PREPARED FOR SUDDEN SQUALLS

AND IF YOU RUN INTO FOG — GIVE ONE LONG BLAST

IF YOU FIND YOURSELF IN SERIOUS TROUBLE - HAVE SOMEONE READY TO BAIL YOU OUT

ABANDON SHIP ONLY AS A LAST RESORT

＊　　　＊　　　＊

"IF ANYONE HEARS THE ENGINE, WE'LL BE OSTRACIZED AT THE CLUB."

GETTING THE WIND UP

THE BEAUFORT SCALE

FORCE 0 DO NOT GET IMPATIENT — YOU COULD BE BECALMED FOR WEEKS

FORCE 1-2   YOU WERE WARNED TO CARRY A SPARE SET OF CHARTS

FORCE 3-4 YOU'RE GLAD SHE BROUGHT HER MOTHER ALONG NOW

FORCE 5-6   — AND MOST OF THAT'S RAW SEWAGE

FORCE 7-8   YOUR DINNER **WAS** IN THE OVEN

FORCE 9-10 IT'S GOING TO BE DICEY GETTING HER HOME UP THE A.1.

FORCE 11-12 DO NOT WORRY - YOUR HOUSE BLEW DOWN ANYWAY

✳   ✳   ✳

" THEY'LL ALLOW ME TO BURY YOU AT SEA BUT NOT IN THESE WATERS, I'M AFRAID "

SEA FEVER

" DO YOU HAVE ANY CAVIAR ? "

"I'M SORRY MATE BUT IT'S A SINGLE-HANDED RACE"

" IF YOU DON'T STOP SLIMMING, I'LL HAVE TO LOOK FOR FRESH CREW "

HELLO! THE CARGO'S SHIFTED

" I DON'T KNOW WHY YOU RACE WHEN YOU'RE SUCH A DAMN POOR LOSER "

" NOW CAN WE START A FAMILY ? "

" MY GOD, JACKSON ! WE'RE NOT GOING TO MAKE IT "

" YOU SINGLE-HANDED CHAPS ARE ALL THE SAME. "

" OH! FOR PITY'S SAKE LET HIM LIGHT IT. "

" THAT WAS A NEAR THING, MAVIS "

" REMEMBER THAT CRUMP AT THE TRAFFIC LIGHTS ? "

" WHAT A STUPID PLACE TO PUT AN OIL RIG ! "

" NAVIGATION'S EASY - JUST FOLLOW THE SEWAGE BACK HOME . "

" YOU CAN ALWAYS TELL WHEN IT'S COWES WEEK "

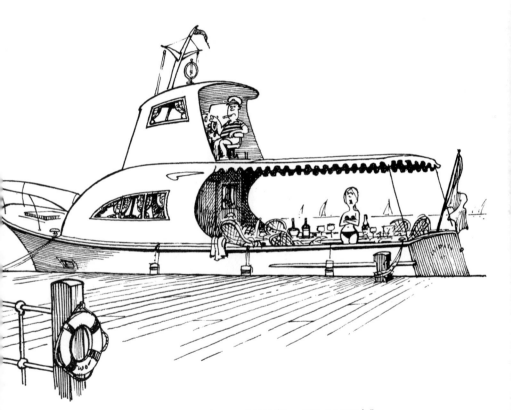

" THE DAILY WOMAN'S LATE AGAIN ! "

" WHO'S WEARING STILETTO HEELS ? "

" HE HATES DOING THE WEEDING. "

" THEY'VE BEEN DONE ! THEY'VE ALL BEEN DONE . "

" KNEE DEEP IN SAWDUST AND SHAVINGS ALL WINTER — AND FOR WHAT ? "